# The Little Red Marble
## A Journey Into Sea Glass

Written by
## Terrilyn Kerr

and illustrated by
## Nancy Perkins

Published by Wood Islands Prints/Tom Schultz; 670 TCH, RR1; Belle River, PE, C0A 1B0; Canada; www.woodislandsprints.com

Terrilyn is a published author and began writing several years ago. She has written a play, poetry and several short stories. This is her first children's book.

She lives on Prince Edward Island and is inspired every day by the sights and sounds of the Island waterways and shores.

terrilynkerr@gmail.com

Nancy Perkins is a painter of nautical themes.

She works in oils and acrylics. The illustrations in the book are in mixed media.

Her work is in Island galleries, private collections and is included in the PEI Provincial Art Bank.

She lives in Montague in the winter and Little Sands in the summer.

nancyperkinspainter@hotmail.com

*The story is dedicated to
the Little Red Marble.*

This is my first children's book and I would like to thank several people who inspired, encouraged and helped make it a reality.

Nancy Perkins, my dear friend and illustrator who has made this book possible.

Will and Julie Yeo

Marian Bruce

Tom Rath

Michael Shumate

Jim Bruce

John Rollins

My wonderful husband, Sandy.

We gratefully acknowledge the financial support of the Southern Kings Arts Council.

This book was written for our grandchildren, James, Jake, Caden, Sophie, Max and Gabby... each one of them has enriched our lives and we look forward to their visits to our home here on this tiny island, cradled in the Atlantic.

A little red marble perched on the edge of a large hole dug in the snow. It shivered with the cold but also with excitement. It was one of hundreds of marbles whose owners were competing in the City Marbles Championship.

Earlier that morning, referees had carefully scooped out a saucer-shaped hole and smoothed the surrounding playing area so that the marbles would roll easily when flicked at the hole from eight feet away. Contestants in the "Bunny-in-the-Hole" competition tried to get their marbles as close to the hole as they could without having them fall in or be knocked in by an opposing marble.

There were marbles from all over the City and the little red marble noticed all the different colours and patterns. There were Alleys made from Alabaster, Cat's Eyes with coloured inserts, Onionskins swirled and layered like an onion, an exotic China of glazed porcelain, Aggies made of agate and the Steelies made of steel. The little red marble was made of a clear, red crystal and was called a Clearie.

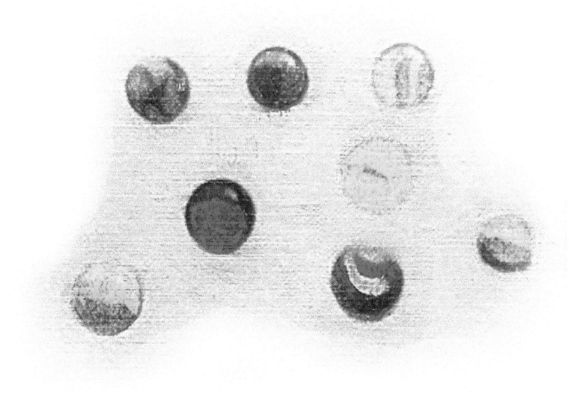

It had been a brutal game. The cold air and frozen ground had caused havoc with some marbles cracking and some shattering after being hit. The little red marble had made it this far without being harmed and now was just one step away from winning the championship.

Patrick, the final contestant, came to the line. The crowd grew silent as he took his place, carefully lined up his prized blue Aggie and, with a flick of his finger, sent it on its way. The blue agate streaked across the snow and with a jarring impact, hit the red marble causing a bright red chip to fly into the air.

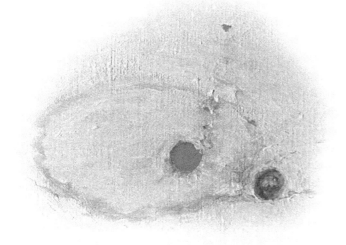

Propelled over the edge and into the hole, the little red marble knew it had lost the championship and it wondered if Patrick would even like it now that it was damaged.

The huge crowd of students pressed around the winner and clapped Patrick on the back. He happily scooped up his prized blue Aggie, the little red marble and all the others he had won, collected his gold medal and ran home to show off his winnings.

As his Mother congratulated him, his little sister Mary came into the kitchen, saw the little, chipped red marble and fell in love.

The little red marble looked up and saw Mary looking at it with longing. It knew then, that it had found a home in her heart. The disappointment that it had been feeling after its loss at the championship game was replaced by a sense of belonging and peace. It had never felt loved in this way before and the little red marble beamed back at Mary. But, Patrick had won it. It was his, and he quickly took the marble to his room.

Patrick kept his treasures in a special drawer and there he placed all of his marbles. He warned Mary to stay away from his room and NEVER touch his things. However, the thought of that wonderful marble waiting for her soon became too much for Mary and she sneaked into Patrick's room. She opened the drawer and picked up the red marble.

Mary saw its soft, warm glow, caressed it and told that sweet marble how beautiful it was. She longed to have it for her own. She also thought that if she did own it, she would never hide the little red marble away but would display it in a place of honour where everyone could admire it.

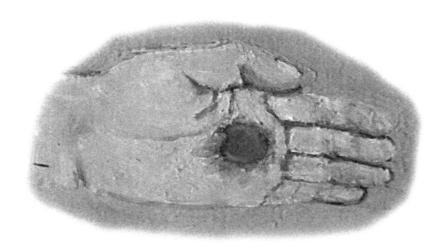

Time passed with Mary looking at and holding the little red marble whenever she could. During those times, the little red marble would also gaze at Mary and beam, letting her know that it loved her too.

Now, when Patrick grew up and finished university, he decided to join the Navy. Over the years he had kept the little red marble and his blue Aggie as his good luck charms. To Mary's dismay, when he left home he took them with him tucked away in his pocket.

One day Patrick's ship was in a fierce storm off the coast of Nova Scotia. Patrick was called to the bridge where the Captain told him to go out into the storm and make sure the forward deck was secure. He put on his gear, buckled himself into his safety harness and went out into the gale. The force of the wind took his breath away and the ship rolled heavily as huge waves crashed onto the deck.

As one powerful wave smashed across the bow, Patrick was knocked off his feet and felt himself sliding toward the edge. But, as the safety harness jerked and held him safe, the little red marble came out of his pocket and fell into the ocean.

The little red marble was shocked as it fell into the icy water and sank into the depths. It seemed to take a long time before it finally settled on the bottom of the ocean floor. It was calmer down on the bottom and the marble was amazed at how different the ocean was compared to the land.

There was motion however, and the little red marble felt itself being moved and tossed over valleys and hills, rocks and flat sandy places. It marvelled at all the different creatures that lived in the ocean. There were lobsters, clams, crabs, squid, scallops and so many different kinds of fish.

Beautiful mermaids swam amongst the swaying seaweed and once, the marble even saw the enormous shadow of a great Blue whale as he passed overhead on his way to the feeding grounds.

As the years rolled on, the little red marble became accustomed to living in the ocean. It learned to love the depths and the different sounds that the sea creatures made as they went along their way.

Because of the constant movement over the bottom of the ocean, the little red marble did notice that it had lost its clear, shiny look and had developed a darker hue, a more elegant, mature look. Throughout its travels, the little red marble never forgot Mary and wondered if it would ever see her again. And always, the marble felt itself moving along the ocean floor towards an unknown destination.

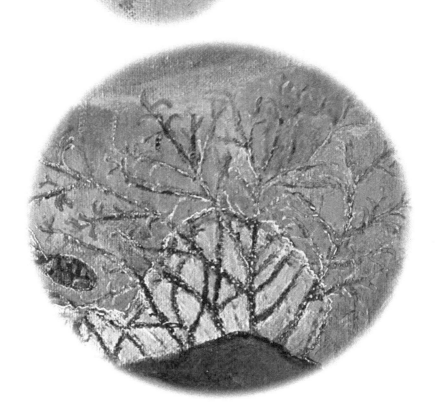

Meanwhile Mary grew up, married and had a family. As busy as she was with her family and career, she never forgot the little red marble and would wonder just where it was. She thought how much she would love to hold it again.

Soon, too soon she thought, her children grew up and had children of their own. She was a grandmother and she rejoiced in the experience. She and her husband retired to a little place called Prince Edward Island on the shores of the Atlantic Ocean. There, Mary learned all about that great body of water and the treasures it held.

One of those treasures was sea glass, beautiful pieces of coloured glassware and dishes that were once used on the great sailing ships that sailed the seas long ago. The glass pieces would have been tossed overboard if they had broken on the voyage. Just like the little red marble, these pieces would have lost their clear look and sharpness and become rounded and pitted by the tumbling action of the ocean, rocks and sand. These same sea glass pieces were much prized by collectors all over the world. Mary learned how to identify these jewels and she would often go to the shore to search for the different colours and shapes of sea glass.

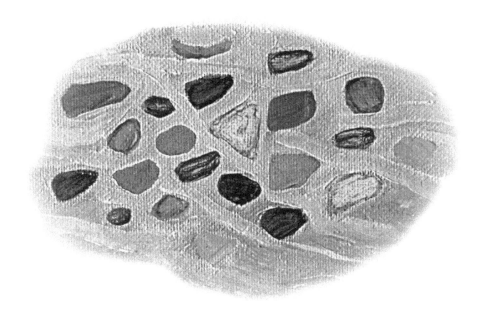

One day when her grandchildren were visiting, Mary took them down to the shore and showed them how to look for sea glass. She taught them to throw the sharp pieces back so those pieces could continue to become more rounded and smooth with the action of the sand and water.

Later that day, as the children ran laughing along the shore, picking up their gems, Mary happened to look down and see the faintest spot of red colour peeking up from the sand. She bent over and picked up a round, red object and as she held it in her hand, a familiar feeling came over her. It was a feeling out of her childhood and she realized with a shock that it was the same feeling she used to get when she held a small, chipped, red marble so long ago.

Could it be? Was it even possible? Mary looked closely at the marble and on its side was a tiny chip. Her heartbeat grew faster as she peered at the marble, looking past the exterior and into the marble's heart.

As the little red marble felt itself lifted up from that sandy shore, it looked up at the grandmother. It suddenly recognized that little girl, Mary, from many years ago. It had travelled for so long along the ocean floor that it had given up hope of ever coming back on to the land. At that moment, the little marble, afraid that Mary might not recognize it, concentrated with all its might and beamed out tiny rays of red light.

As Mary saw the tiny beams of light she knew then without a doubt, there in her hand was the very same little marble of her childhood. Tears of joy filled her eyes as she gazed on the lovely, once-lost treasure.

Rejoicing, she called her grandchildren and began to tell them the incredible story of that little red marble and its remarkable journey. Later she thought, when winter came, she would use her precious red marble to teach them the game of "Bunny-in-the-Hole".

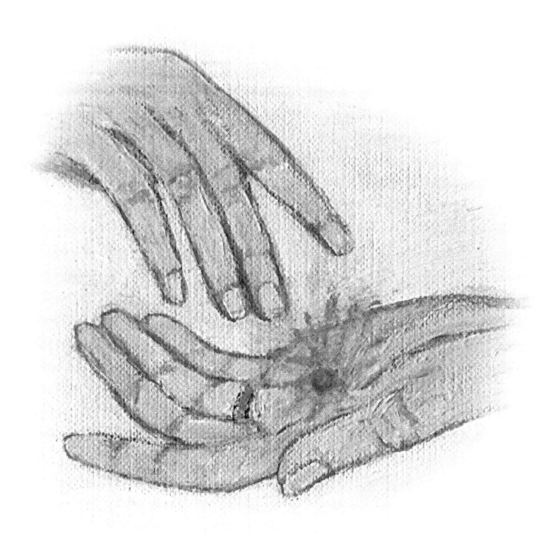

And that little red marble? Well, it glowed with happiness and felt a lasting peace as it finally rested in its place of honour in Mary's living room.

Lightning Source UK Ltd.
Milton Keynes UK
UKHW050247220122
397529UK00005B/81